HOLIDAY
PARTIES

JUDITH STREB

HOLIDAY PARTIES

DISCARD

Franklin Watts/New York/London/Toronto/Sydney/1985

To my parents,
Margaret and Raymond Streb.
Thank you for making
every holiday
a very special occasion.

ILLUSTRATIONS BY
ANNE CANEVARI GREEN

Library of Congress Cataloging in Publication Data

Streb, Judith.
Holiday parties.

Bibliography: p.
Includes index.
Summary: Describes the origins and symbols of
Valentine's Day, Halloween, Thanksgiving, Christmas,
and Hanukkah, and suggests decorations and activities
for parties celebrating these holidays.
1. Children's parties—Juvenile literature. 2. Holidays
—United States—Juvenile literature. [1. Parties.
2. Holidays]   I. Green, Anne Canevari, ill. II. Title.
GV1205.S88 1985   793.2'1   85-8806
ISBN 0-531-10041-3

CONTENTS

HOLIDAY
PARTIES

CHAPTER ONE

HOLIDAYS ARE SPECIAL DAYS

Holiday is defined in the dictionary as a religious feast day, a day free from work, a period of time for recreation and rest, or a day fixed by law for the closing of businesses. But we know holidays as days for family gatherings, celebrations with friends, decorations, special meals, gift giving, card sending, and wonderful memories.

From the earliest of times, people have thought of many reasons to celebrate. Some of these celebrations became traditional. Many of our holidays, such as Christmas, St. Patrick's Day, and Yom Kippur, are of a religious origin. Some holidays, such as the Fourth of July, Flag Day, Memorial Day, Lincoln's Birthday, and Veterans Day, are of a patriotic nature. Other days have meaning to people because of a general need. Because the family unit is very important to society, we celebrate our mothers, fathers, and grandparents by setting aside special days to honor them. We even have a day on which we determine if we will have six more weeks of winter, depending on whether or not a little groundhog sees its shadow.

Regardless of the reason for wanting to celebrate, we all look forward to special occasions. The time during which we anticipate and prepare for a holiday can be special indeed.

Five major holidays in the United States are Valentine's Day, Halloween, Thanksgiving, Christmas, and Hanukkah. If you are planning a party to celebrate one of these holidays, this book will help you. You will learn about the origin of each holiday along with the meaning of the symbols connected with it. You will be given ideas for invitations, place mats, place cards, party favors, room and door decorations, refreshments and games.

Detailed directions and illustrations are supplied for the construction of each decoration. Recipes for tasty refreshments are suggested. The directions for playing all games are also given.

A successful party doesn't usually just happen. It requires thought and preparation. Here are some guidelines to help you in your planning:

■ Develop a party theme, a reason to celebrate.
■ Decide on a date, time, and place for your party. Make or buy your party invitations, and send them about two weeks in advance. If you are planning a party for the classroom, you will have no problems knowing whether or not your guests will come. But if you are planning a home party, you should request some kind of response from the people you have invited so that you will know exactly who is coming, how many refreshments to prepare, and what types of activities to plan. Even if you are planning a family celebration, it is nice to know which aunts, uncles, cousins, and grandparents will definitely be there. Design your invitation so that your guests will know in advance the type of party it will be. If you want to give special instructions to your guests, such as to wear a costume or bring a swimsuit, write them on the invitation.
■ Plan the decorations for the party. They can be simple ones, such as streamers hanging from the ceiling along with a few balloons, to very fancy decorations, with place mats and place cards on the tables and a party favor for each guest to take home as a remembrance of a good time.
■ Refreshments are always an important part of every party. It seems as though everyone always remembers what he or she ate at a party! You will want to plan a drink and a snack or maybe even a meal for your guests. Whatever you decide to serve, make sure you prepare enough. Well in advance of the party, take a good look at the recipes you plan to use, and be sure to buy all the necessary ingredients.
■ Think of party activities that reflect the theme. Decide on games you will play and prizes you will award.

Since special parties require so much preparation and planning, you might wish to use the following checklist so that nothing is forgotten during the planning stages.

─────────── **PARTY CHECKLIST** ───────────

☐ Decide on a party theme.
☐ Choose a date, time, and place for the party.
☐ Make or buy invitations.
☐ Make a party guest list.
☐ Address the invitations.
☐ Send the invitations.
☐ Decide on party decorations.
☐ Make a list of party supplies to buy, such as paper tablecloths, plates, drinking cups, and napkins.
☐ Make a list of supplies you already have on hand, such as flatware.
☐ Make a list of decorations to buy or make, such as place cards, table decorations, place mats, room decorations, party favors, and door decorations.
☐ Write a list of guests who are coming to the party.
☐ Decide what refreshments you will serve.
☐ Gather your recipes to make a grocery list.
☐ Shop for the ingredients.
☐ Make a list of your party foods and check them off as they are prepared.
☐ Buy your party supplies.
☐ Collect the necessary dishes and flatware you will need.
☐ Buy or make the decorations.
☐ Decide on games to play at the party.
☐ Collect or make all necessary equipment to play the games.
☐ Buy or make the prizes that will be awarded.

The day has finally arrived! Your guests are about to arrive. If you have planned carefully, and your list has been checked and double-checked, then you will be ready for your guests to come and have a grand time.

One final note: Parties are fun for everyone and are a wonderful excuse to relax from schoolwork or jobs. You really do not need a holiday to have a party. Think of some other reasons to celebrate. Start your own traditions with family or friends. You can adapt some of the ideas in this book for your own special celebrations and memorable times. Happy partying!

CHAPTER TWO

A cupid, a heart, and a dove,
And a sweet little message of love—
  Oh, that's what I got
  For the one who a lot
Of this day I have spent thinking ove.

On Valentine's Day, which is celebrated each year on February 14, people send greetings of love to each other.

The origin of the holiday is uncertain. According to one story there once lived a Roman emperor named Claudius who thought that single men made better soldiers. So he issued a law that made it impossible for young men to marry. A priest named Valentine disobeyed the ruler and married young couples in secret.

According to another story, in the reign of this same pagan emperor there lived a Christian named Valentine who was very friendly with the children in his town. Because of his religion, he was put in prison. The children missed their friend very much, so they would write loving letters to him and slip them through the bars of his prison cell. Thus began the sending of valentines.

The custom of sending valentine cards has grown through the years. Millions of people in the United States as well as other countries send special greetings or gifts of candy or flowers to express love or friendship on this day.

THE SYMBOLS OF VALENTINE'S DAY

The cards or candy boxes are decorated with lace and symbols such as hearts, cupids, and flowers. They have special meanings.

The *heart* is necessary for life. At one time it was believed that the heart was the center of our feelings. Because feelings of love were supposed to come from the heart, people used the heart as a symbol of affection.

In Greek mythology *Cupid* was the son of Venus. Cupid was called the god of love. According to the myth, Cupid's magic arrows made both gods and people fall in love.

Because of their beauty, *flowers* have been important to poets, artists, lovers, and nations as emblems, and even to soldiers who have worn them on badges to symbolize victory.

PARTY PLANS

INVITATIONS

Heart Cards

Materials

    Sheets of red, pink, or white construction paper

    Pieces of wrapping paper, wallpaper, or foil

    Yarn, Glue, Scissors, Felt-tip pens

Directions

1. Cut the construction paper into 6″ × 9″ (15 × 23 cm) pieces.
2. Fold each piece of construction paper in half to form a card.
3. To decorate the front of each card, cut heart shapes from wrapping paper, wallpaper, or foil. Cut a different heart for each card.
4. Glue the heart on the front.
5. Glue a yarn bow on the heart.

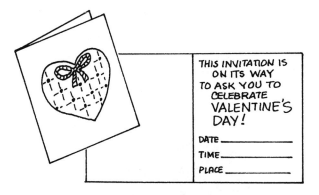

6. On the inside of the invitation, use a felt-tip pen to write a verse.

    If this is a home party, also include your name, address, and phone number.

Fold-Out Hearts

Materials

    Red or pink construction paper

    Pencil, Scissors, Felt-tip pen

Directions

1. Cut red or pink construction paper into 12″ × 3½″ (30 × 9 cm) pieces.
2. Fold the paper in half three times.
3. Draw half of a heart on the top piece as shown.

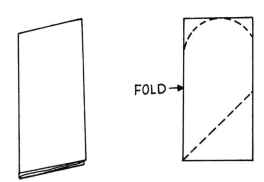

4. Cut only on the dotted lines.
5. Open the hearts and use a felt-tip pen to write your party invitation on them. Include the date, time, and place of the party.
6. Make one invitation for each invited guest.

TABLE DECORATIONS

Heart Collage Place Mats

Materials

    Pieces of red or white construction paper, 12" × 18" (30 × 45 cm)
    Scraps of wrapping paper, wallpaper, construction paper, colorful magazine pages
    Scissors, Glue
    Clear contact paper (optional)

Directions

1. For each place mat, cut several different-sized hearts from paper of different patterns and colors (wrapping paper, wallpaper, construction paper, magazine pages).
2. Overlap the hearts as you glue them on the large sheet of red or white construction paper.
3. Cover each place mat with clear contact paper, if you wish. This will allow you to wipe off any spills.
4. Make one place mat for each place setting.

If the party is for the classroom, the place mats could be made during an art class the week before the party.

Woven Heart Place Mats

Materials

    Sheets of red and white construction paper, 12" × 18" (30 × 45 cm)
    Scissors, Glue, Pencil

Directions

1. Use one sheet of red and one sheet of white construction paper for each place mat. Round off one 12" (30 cm) side on each sheet by cutting.

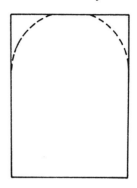

2. Cut slits in each heart half. Begin at the straight 12" edge (30 cm), and cut slits that are 12" (30 cm) long and 1" (3 cm) wide.

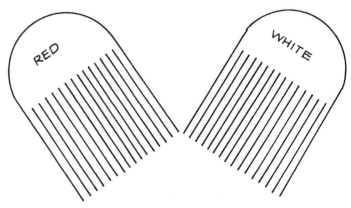

3. Place each half at an angle and weave the two halves together.
4. Glue all the ends down.
5. Make one place mat for each place setting.

Heart Napkin Ring

Materials

Red, white, or pink construction paper

Pipe cleaners, Scissors, Glue

Directions

1. For each napkin ring, cut a 2'' (6 cm) heart from red construction paper.
2. Poke two small holes in the center of the heart.
3. Push a pipe cleaner through one hole and out the other.

4. Twist the two ends of the pipe cleaner together to form a ring.
5. To cover the pipe cleaner on the front of the heart, glue a smaller heart of pink or white over it.
6. Make one napkin ring for each place setting.

Valentine Napkin Rings

Materials

Red, white, or pink construction paper

Scissors, Glue

Directions

1. For each napkin ring, cut a 5'' × 1'' (13 × 3 cm) strip of construction paper. Glue the ends to form a ring.

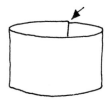

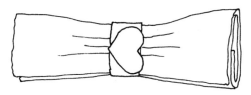

2. Cut a heart from construction paper and glue it on the front of the ring.
3. Roll a napkin lengthwise and stick it inside the ring.
4. Make one napkin ring for each place setting.

Cut-out Place Cards

Materials

Red construction paper

Scissors, Pencil, Felt-tip pen

Directions

1. For each place card, cut a piece of red construction paper 4½'' × 6'' (11 × 15 cm) in size.
2. Fold the construction paper in half with the 4½'' sides meeting.
3. Draw the outline of a heart with a place for a name at the bottom.
4. Cut only on the dotted lines.

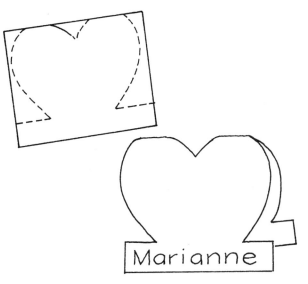

5. Write the guest's name at the bottom of the heart with a felt-tip pen.
6. Stand the heart up.
7. Make one place card for each guest.

[9]

Valentine Place Cards

Materials
White index cards, 3″ × 5″ (7½ × 13 cm)
Felt-tip pen
Valentine stickers

Directions
1. For each place card, fold the index card in half with the 3″ (7½ cm) sides meeting.
2. Glue the sticker in one corner.
3. Write the guest's name next to it.
4. Make one place card for each guest.

Table Centerpiece

Materials
Flower pot or coffee can
Styrofoam block or sand
Red ribbon
Green pipe cleaners or thin wire
Construction paper
Tape, Scissors
Felt-tip pens or crayons

Directions
1. For each centerpiece, fill an empty flower pot or coffee can with a Styrofoam block or with sand.
2. Tie a red bow around the pot.
3. Cut several different sizes of hearts from construction paper of different colors.
4. Decorate the hearts, using felt-tip pens or crayons.
5. Tape each heart to a green pipe cleaner or to wire.
6. Place the hearts in the pot.

PARTY FAVORS

Valentine Pockets

Materials
Red construction paper
Scissors, Glue
Lace, yard, valentine stickers (optional)
Valentine cards

Directions
1. For each Valentine Pocket, cut two 6″ (15 cm) hearts from red construction paper.
2. Put a small amount of glue along the bottom edge of one heart.
3. Place the second heart on top of the glued heart. Allow time for the glue to dry. The opening at the top of the two hearts forms a pocket.
4. Decorate the outside of the Valentine Pocket with lace, yarn, or valentine stickers, if you wish.
5. Make a Valentine Pocket for each guest and place a special valentine card inside. If the party guests are exchanging valentines, the cards can be placed inside each guest's Valentine Pocket.

Lollipop Hearts

Materials

Red construction paper
Tape
Yarn
Scissors
Lollipops

Directions

1. For each Lollipop Heart, cut a 6" (15 cm) heart from red construction paper.
2. Tie a yarn bow around a lollipop.
3. Tape the lollipop to the center of the heart.
4. Make a Lollipop Heart for each guest.

ROOM DECORATIONS

Several different decorations can be made to hang around the room. Use various heart designs to decorate walls, doors, windows, chairs, etc.

Heart-shaped Butterfly

Materials

Wooden clothespins
Red, pink, white, and black construction paper
Pipe cleaners, Glue, Scissors
Black paint, Paint brushes

Directions

1. Paint each clothespin with the black paint. These will be the bodies of the butterflies.
2. For each clothespin, cut two 3" (8 cm) and two 1" (3 cm) hearts from red construction paper. These will be the side and the bottom wings.
3. Cut smaller hearts from pink, white, or black construction paper to glue on the wings to form a pattern.

4. Glue all four wings onto the clothespin.
5. Glue two pipe cleaners to the top of the clothespin for the butterfly's antennae. Glue a small heart on the tip of each antenna.

6. Attach the butterflies to windows and doors or suspend them from the ceiling with thread.

Valentine Wreath

Materials

Cardboard or pizza circle
Construction paper, wallpaper, wrapping paper
Scissors, Glue

Directions

1. For one wreath, cut a large ring from cardboard or from a pizza circle, about 18" (45 cm) in diameter.
2. Cut several different-sized hearts from different colored and textured paper.
3. Glue the hearts on the ring.
4. Hang the wreath on a door.

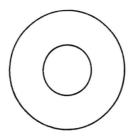 

[11]

Valentine Streamer

Materials

Red and pink construction paper
Felt-tip pen
Ribbon or yarn
Scissors

Directions

1. For one streamer, cut nineteen 6″ (15 cm) hearts from red construction paper and two hearts from pink paper.
2. Make two small holes at the top of each heart.
3. Write one letter on each red heart to spell the words HAPPY VALENTINE'S DAY. Do not forget the apostrophe on one heart.
4. Cut a piece of ribbon or yarn. Thread it through the hearts that spell HAPPY. Next thread a pink heart. Then thread VALENTINE'S, another pink heart, and then DAY.
5. Tie a bow at each end and hang the streamer for the guests to see.

Ruffled Valentine

Materials

Red construction paper
White crepe paper streamers
Glue
Scissors
Felt-tip pens

Directions

1. For each Ruffled Valentine, cut two large red hearts, about 9″ (23 cm) wide.

2. To make the ruffle for the heart, cut a piece of white crepe paper streamer long enough to fit around one heart.
3. Glue the white crepe paper around the edge of one heart.
4. Glue the second heart over the heart with the ruffle.

5. Use a felt-tip pen to write a valentine message on the ruffled heart.
6. Make several hearts to hang around the room.

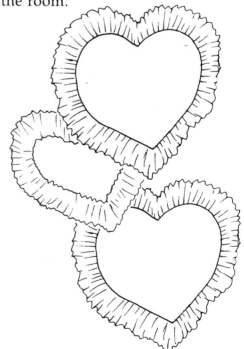

REFRESHMENTS

Party Punch

Serve a red fruit punch at the party. Use Hawaiian Punch or one of the cranberry drinks.

Kool Punch

Ginger ale
Cherry or strawberry Kool Aid (one package)

1. Prepare the Kool Aid according to the directions on the package.
2. Pour the Kool Aid into ice cube trays. Allow to freeze.
3. Place a few flavored ice cubes in a glass and fill with ginger ale.

Hearty Sandwiches

White bread
Strawberry or raspberry jam

1. Use a cookie cutter to cut heart shapes from the bread. Discard crusts.
2. Spread a red-colored jam on one slice of bread and top with a second slice.

Valentine Cookies

2/3 cup (150 ml) margarine
1 3/4 cup (435 ml) sugar
2 eggs, well beaten
1/2 teaspoon (2.5 ml) vanilla
3 cups (750 ml) flour
2 teaspoons (10 ml) baking powder
1/2 teaspoon (2.5 ml) salt
Red candy hearts or cherries

1. Preheat the oven to 425°F (220°C).
2. Cream the sugar and margarine until fluffy.
3. Stir in the two well-beaten eggs.
4. Add vanilla.
5. Sift together the flour, baking powder, and salt.
6. Blend dry ingredients into the creamed mixture and mix together thoroughly.
7. Drop by teaspoons on a lightly greased baking sheet.
8. Place a cherry in the center of each cookie. (If you use candy hearts, put them on the warm cookies as they come out of the oven.)
9. Bake for 8 to 10 minutes.

Hearty Ice Cream Delight

Vanilla ice cream or yogurt
Candy hearts

1. Place a scoop or two of ice cream into each dish.
2. Sprinkle candy hearts on top.

GAMES

Heart Bingo

Make special bingo cards, but write the letters H E A R T across the top of the card rather than B I N G O. Play the game the same way as bingo.

H	E	A	R	T
8	17	28	52	62
6	21	31	48	69
9	19	♥	61	3
11	6	39	59	75
1	16	40	47	64

[13]

Hearts in a Jar

1. Before your guests arrive, fill a clear jar with candy hearts. Be sure to count the number of candy pieces.
2. As the guests arrive, have them write on pieces of paper their names and the number of hearts they think are in the jar.
3. Some time during the party tell the guests the exact number of candy pieces and give a prize to the person who guessed the closest number without going over the amount.

Mend a Broken Heart

1. For this game the guests will work as partners.
2. For each pair of players you will need to cut a large heart from construction paper. Then cut each heart in half, leaving a jagged edge.
3. One player pins one half of the heart on a bulletin board or tapes one half to a door.
4. The partner is blindfolded, and tries to match his or her half to the one on the board or door.
5. The partner is allowed to guide the blindfolded player by giving verbal directions, such as, "Move right" or "Go down a little."
6. The players that form the most perfect heart win the game.

Heart Toss

1. You will need two baskets or boxes for this game. You may want to tie a red ribbon around the basket or cover the box with red paper.
2. You will also need a bag of candy hearts.
3. Divide the party guests into two teams.
4. The team members will work in pairs.
5. A player from each team will be given six candy hearts.
6. A second player from each team will hold the basket or box.
7. The players on each team are to stand 6' (2 m) apart.
8. The player with the hearts is to throw the candy into the container held by the other team member.
9. The container can be moved to catch the hearts.
10. One point is given for each heart caught.
11. When six hearts have been thrown, two new team members play until all the guests have played.
12. At the end of the game tally the scores to determine which team has won.

Red Things Game

1. Give each player a piece of paper and a pencil.
2. Tell the players to think of as many things as they can that are red.
3. When you give the signal, have the players write down these things.
4. At the end of the given time period (allow about 5 minutes), check what the players have written.
5. The player with the most responses is the winner.

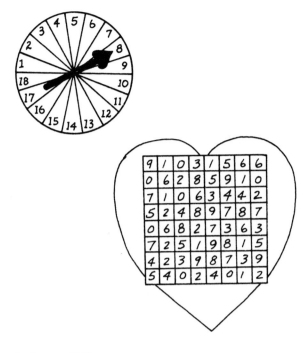

Spin to Win

1. The game requires the making of a spinner and game cards.
2. The spinner should have eighteen sections. Write the numerals one through eighteen, one per section of the spinner as shown.
3. Each player will need a game card. Block the card off into 64 sections. Randomly write the numerals *0* through *9*, one numeral per section, until the card is filled. Each game card must be different.
4. To play the game, the leader will spin the spinner.
5. Have the players use popcorn kernels to block out or cover any two numerals whose sums equal the number shown on the spinner.
6. The first player to block off an entire row, vertically or horizontally, wins the game.
7. This game could be played at a party with any theme. To keep with the valentine theme, back each playing card with a large red heart.

Scrambled Hearts

1. Make a list of words that have the word *heart* in them. For example: *hearty, heartsick, heartland, hearth, heartbroken, heartstrings, heartless, heartthrob, heartburn, heartfelt, heartache, heartily.*
2. Cut several small hearts from red construction paper.
3. For each heart word, write one letter on each heart to spell the word.
4. Then scramble the hearts and place the scrambled word into an envelope. Do this for all the heart words.
5. Divide the guests into two teams and seat them around a table.
6. Give each team member an envelope.

7. At the signal to begin, each player is to open the envelope and unscramble the word.
8. Since the players are working in teams, the players can help each other.
9. The first team to have all the words unscrambled wins.

CHAPTER THREE

HALLOWEEN

Out tonight for trick or treat,
Halloweeners roam the street.
Bats and ghosts fly through the air,
Witches, goblins everywhere.
Costumed beggars on the run,
Playing tricks to have some fun.
Jack-o'-lanterns glowing bright
On this spooky, festive night.

Halloween is a fun-filled holiday with its costumes, trick-or-treating, and ghosts and goblins of the night. Halloween is celebrated annually on October 31. Children wear costumes and visit neighboring houses to beg for treats. Many people decorate their windows with carved jack-o'-lanterns glowing by the light of a candle burning inside.

THE SYMBOLS OF HALLOWEEN

Costumes, ghosts, witches, goblins, fortune-telling—these symbols probably all date back to a festival that was held over 2,000 years ago by a group of people known as the Celts. The Celts lived in England, Ireland, and Scotland. On the evening of the feast the Celts would burn crops and animals as a sacrifice to the evil powers so that no harm would come to them. Sometimes some of the people would dress in costume and tell fortunes about the future.

Other costume-wearing customs originated in countries such as Ireland, Scotland, and Wales. People would dress in costumes and march in parades to beg for food. Or people would dress in costume to scare away witches and other harmful spirits. The celebration of Halloween became popular in the United States around the 1800s with the coming of immigrants from the British Isles.

A *jack-o'-lantern* is made by carving out a pumpkin, putting a face on the pumpkin, and a lighted candle inside. The original lanterns of many years ago were actually carved-out potatoes, turnips, or beets.

PARTY PLANS

INVITATIONS

Haunted House Invitations

Materials
Yellow and black construction paper
Scissors
White crayon
Felt-tip pen
Glue

Directions
1. For each haunted house, cut a sheet of construction paper into a piece 9″ × 6″ (23 × 15 cm) in size.
2. Draw and cut the outline shape of a haunted house.
3. With a white crayon, draw a front door and at least two large windows. See the illustration for ideas. Add more details later.
4. Cut on three sides of each door and window so the door and windows can be opened and the paper folded back.
5. Place the haunted house on a sheet of yellow construction paper and trace the outline of the house. Cut out the yellow house.
6. Attach the yellow house to the back of the black house with glue. Allow the glue to dry.
7. Inside each window and door that can be opened write your party information: date, time, place, and any special instructions, such as to wear a costume.

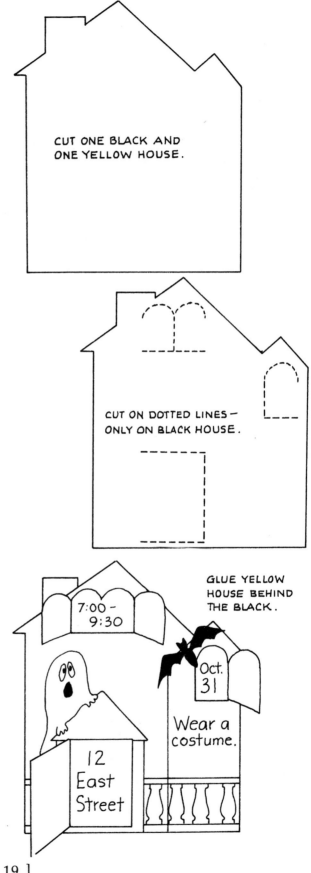

CUT ONE BLACK AND ONE YELLOW HOUSE.

CUT ON DOTTED LINES — ONLY ON BLACK HOUSE.

GLUE YELLOW HOUSE BEHIND THE BLACK.

7:00 – 9:30

Oct. 31

Wear a costume.

12 East Street

[19]

Jack-o'-lantern Invitations

Materials
Orange construction paper
Felt-tip pens or crayons
Scissors

Directions
1. For each jack-o'-lantern invitation, cut a piece of orange construction paper 9″ × 6″ (23 × 15 cm) in size.
2. Fold the paper in half with the 6″ sides meeting, and draw the shape of a pumpkin on the front. The left side of the pumpkin is drawn on the fold.

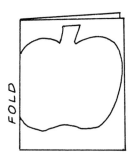

3. Cut out the pumpkin shape while the paper is still folded, taking care not to cut on the fold.
4. Draw a jack-o'-lantern face on the front of the card, using felt-tip pens or crayons. Make the face on each invitation different.
5. Inside the card write your party invitation. You may wish to write a verse.

Witches, ghosts, and goblins
Make such a scary sight!
Wear a spooky costume,
and join us
Halloween night.
Place
Time

TABLE DECORATIONS

Spooky Place Mats

Materials
Orange and black construction paper, 12″ × 18″ (30 × 45 cm)
Scissors
Black felt-tip pen
Yellow crayon

Directions
1. For each place mat, you will need one sheet of orange construction paper from which you will cut the shape of the largest pumpkin possible.
2. Make a jack-o'-lantern face on the pumpkin, using a black felt-tip pen.

3. An alternative would be to draw a large cat on the black construction paper.
4. Color a pair of yellow eyes on the cat.
5. Make one mat for each guest.

[20]

Witch's Hat Place Cards

Materials
- Black and orange construction paper
- Scissors
- Glue
- Black felt-tip pen

Directions
1. For each place card, use a piece of black construction paper that is 7" × 3" (18 × 7½ cm). Fold the paper in half with the 3" (7½ cm) sides meeting.
2. Draw the outline of a witch's hat, beginning with the point of the hat at the fold of the paper. Make the width of this point about ½" (1 cm) wide so that when the hat is cut out, the two parts will be held together at the point.
3. With the paper still folded, cut out the hat, taking care not to cut on the fold.
4. Glue a band cut from orange construction paper on the hat.
5. Use a black felt-tip pen to write the party guest's name on the hatband.
6. Make a witch's hat place card for each guest.

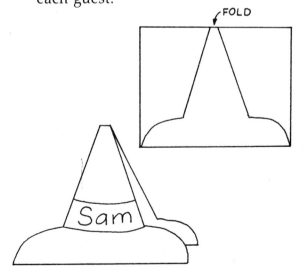

Spooky Place Cards

Materials
- White paper
- Black felt-tip pen
- Scissors
- Drinking straws
- Tape

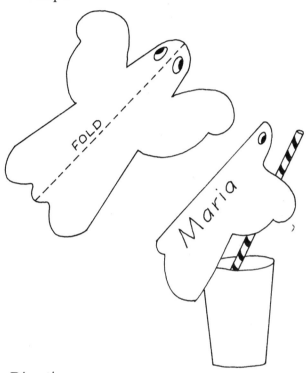

Directions
1. For each place card, cut a piece of white paper 4" (10 cm) square.
2. Fold the paper in half. Draw half a ghost with its back on the fold.
3. Cut out the ghost, careful not to cut on the fold.
4. Draw eyes with a black felt-tip pen, and write the guest's name on one half of the ghost.
5. Crease the ghost. Use a piece of tape or a drop of glue to attach the ghost's arms to a drinking straw and place it in a drinking cup. If it is attached low enough, it will not interfere with drinking.
6. Make a place card for each guest.

Spooky Napkin Rings

Materials
    Black and orange construction paper
    Scissors

Directions
1. For each napkin ring, cut a pumpkin from the orange construction paper or a cat from the black. Each shape should be about 3" (8 cm) square.

2. Cut a hole about 1" (3 cm) in diameter in the center of each shape.
3. Pull the napkin through the hole.

Carved Jack-o'-lantern

Materials
    Pumpkin
    Knife (a butter knife will do)
    Crayon, Spoon, Candle

Directions
1. Buy a pumpkin that is nicely shaped.
2. Carve around the stem and remove the lid.
3. Scoop out the pulp and seeds.
4. Draw a face on the pumpkin, using a crayon. Carefully use a knife to carve out the face.
5. Place the carved pumpkin on a table. Place a candle inside.
6. At party time, dim the lights and light the candle.

Jack-around-a-bowl Centerpiece

Materials
    Orange construction paper
    Scissors, Tape

Directions
1. For each bowl you will be using for refreshments, cut a strip of orange construction paper 4" (10 cm) wide and long enough to wrap around the bowl. You may have to tape strips of construction paper together so that the band will be long enough.
2. Fold the paper, accordion-style, into as many sections as you can, making each section at least 3" (7½ cm) wide.

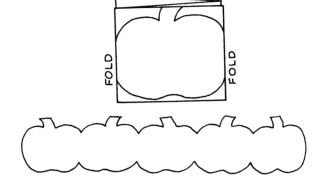

3. On the top square draw the outline shape of a pumpkin, making the sides of the pumpkin touch the sides of the paper.
4. With the paper still folded, cut out the pumpkin shape, leaving the sides on the fold uncut so that the pumpkins will be joined together.
5. Unfold the pumpkins. Wrap the string of jack-o'-lanterns around a bowl of refreshments and tape the two end pumpkins together.

[22]

PARTY FAVORS

Nut and Candy Cups

Materials

    Cupcake papers
    Orange, black,
      or white con-
      struction paper
    Stapler
    Scissors
    Nuts and candy

Directions

1. For each nut and candy cup, cut an orange jack-o'-lantern, a black cat, or a white ghost from construction paper. Make each shape about 2″ (5 cm) square.
2. Staple the shape on the front of a cupcake paper.
3. Fill the cup with nuts and candy.
4. Make a cup for each guest.

Tasty Pumpkin Favors

Materials

    Apples or oranges
    Orange crepe paper, Green yarn
    Black felt-tip pen

Directions

1. For each favor, wrap an orange or an apple in a piece of crepe paper.
2. Gather the crepe paper at the top and twist.
3. Tie with a piece of green yarn.
4. If you wish, color a face on the pumpkin, using a black felt-tip pen.
5. Make one favor for each guest.

ROOM DECORATIONS

Hanging Spiders

Materials

    Black construction paper
    Black yarn, Tape, Glue, Scissors

Directions

1. Cut pieces of black construction paper, 4″ × 6″ (10 × 15 cm) in size.
2. Draw a spider shape (head and body) on one piece of paper. Place the second sheet of paper underneath.
3. Cut out the spider, keeping the two sheets of paper together. You will have two identical spider shapes.
4. Cut four lengths of black yarn, each about 10″ (25 cm) long.
5. Lay the pieces of yarn, side by side, over one spider. Tape the yarn in place.

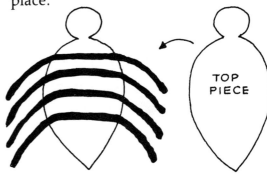

6. Glue the second spider shape over the yarn. The yarn will be glued between the two spider shapes.
7. Tape another piece of yarn to the top of the spider. Suspend the spider from the ceiling or doorway.

Window Jack-o'-lanterns

Materials

Orange construction paper, 9″ ×
   12″ (23 × 30 cm) in size
Yellow cellophane or tissue paper
Scissors, Tape, Glue

Directions

1. Fold a piece of construction paper in half with the 9″ sides meeting.
2. Draw half a pumpkin shape.
3. Cut out the pumpkin.
4. While the paper is still folded, cut out eyes, nose, and mouth.
5. Using your cut-out pumpkin as a pattern, cut out a second identical pumpkin and face.
6. Place a piece of yellow cellophane or tissue paper over one of the jack-o'-lantern faces and tape in place.

CUT OUT TWO
JACK-O-LANTERNS.

FOLD

TAPE THE YELLOW
CELLOPHANE OR TISSUE
PAPER OVER THE FACE.

GLUE THE SECOND
CUT-OUT ON TOP
WITH THE CELLOPHANE
OR TISSUE IN BETWEEN.

7. Then glue the two jack-o'-lantern halves together with the yellow paper between them.
8. Tape the jack-o'-lantern to the window. The jack-o'-lantern will appear to glow when sunlight shines through the cellophane or tissue.

Ghost Host

Materials

Floor lamp with lampshade
Black construction paper
White sheet
Bucket
Yardstick
Gloves
Hat

Directions

1. Place a floor lamp in a spot where your Ghost Host can greet your guests.
2. Turn a bucket upside down over the lampshade.
3. Place a yardstick across the top of the shade below the bucket.
4. Drape a sheet over the lamp, bucket, and yardstick.
5. Put a glove on each end of the yardstick. The gloves will look like hands, and will also hold the stick in place.
6. Cut two black circles for eyes and pin them to the sheet.
7. Put a hat on top of the ghost's head.
8. If you turn on the lamp, the Ghost Host will glow.

HALLOWEEN COSTUMES

Your party can be decorated with the guests if they are all dressed in costumes. You may wish to have a definite theme for the costumes, such as monsters, witches, outer-space creatures, animals, characters from literature or history, food items, or toys. Give your party guests plenty of notice so they will have time to make their costumes. A variation would be to request that each guest wear a mask. It would be fun to guess who each masked guest is as he or she arrives.

REFRESHMENTS

Cinnamon Cider

Apple cider
Cinnamon sticks

1. Warm the apple cider.
2. When you are ready to serve, put a cinnamon stick in each cup of hot cider.

Hot Cocoa

Use packets of instant cocoa made with hot water or warm milk. Top each cup of cocoa with a marshmallow.

Orange-Apple Punch

1 6-ounce (177 ml) can of frozen orange juice concentrate, thawed
1 6-ounce (177 ml) can frozen lemonade concentrate, thawed
1 quart (.95 l) apple juice, chilled
1 large bottle of ginger ale, chilled
1 pint (473 ml) orange sherbet

1. Mix the concentrates and the apple juice in a large bowl.
2. Just before serving add the ginger ale.
3. Spoon in scoops of orange sherbet.

Pumpkin Cheese-wiches

Slices of yellow American cheese
Rye bread
Olives

1. Cut pumpkin shapes from the slices of cheese, using a cookie cutter.
2. Place the cheese pumpkins on slices of rye bread.
3. Add the other ingredients. Mix.
4. Place in the oven just long enough for the cheese to begin to melt.

Deviled Eggs

6 hard-boiled eggs
½ teaspoon (2.5 ml) salt
½ teaspoon (2.5 ml) dry mustard
¼ teaspoon (1.2 ml) pepper
3 tablespoons (45 ml) mayonnaise
Olives, bacon bits (optional)

1. Cut the peeled eggs in half lengthwise.
2. Remove and mash the yolks.
3. Add the rest of the ingredients. Mix.
4. Heap the egg mixture into each egg white.
5. Top with bacon bits or olive slices.

Orange Snack Cups

1 3-ounce package orange Jell-O gelatin
Miniature marshmallows
Sliced fruit

1. Follow the directions on the package for making the Jell-O. Mix the Jell-O in a pitcher.
2. Pour the gelatin into paper cups.
3. Place a few marshmallows and fruit slices into each cup and stir.
4. Put the paper cups on a tray and place in the refrigerator. Leave until firm.
5. Makes about 6 servings.

Pumpkin in a Hole

Chocolate donuts (or plain donuts)
Orange sherbet
Candy corn or jelly beans

1. Fill the hole of each donut with a large scoop of orange sherbet.
2. Make a pumpkin face in the sherbet with the candy corn and jelly beans.

GAMES

Jack-o'-lantern Toss

1. Make five paper jack-o'-lanterns by wadding up newspaper and wrapping orange crepe paper around it.
2. Twist the crepe paper at the top and secure it with a piece of string or a rubberband.
3. Make a different face on each jack-o'-lantern, using a black felt-tip pen.
4. Set the five jack-o'-lanterns in a row at the back edge of a table.

5. Give each player five small balls or beanbags to use to throw and try to knock the jack-o'-lanterns off the table.
6. Give a ribbon or small prize to each player who is able to knock off all five.

Halloween Words

1. Divide your guests into teams of three players each.
2. Give each team a sheet of paper with the word 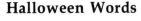HALLOWEEN written at the top.
3. At the signal to begin, each team is to write as many words as they can, using only those letters that appear in the word *Halloween.* The letters can be used more than once.
4. At the end of five minutes (or longer if you wish), have the teams count the number of words written. Check for spelling.
5. The team with the most correctly spelled words wins the game.

Apple Bobbing

1. Fill a large tub with water and float apples in it.
2. Allow the guests to take turns trying to get an apple, using only their mouths and teeth.
3. Each guest who successfully removes an apple from the tub of water, using only the teeth, gets to eat the apple. You may want to time each player and award a prize to the player who gets the apple the fastest.

Count the Corn

1. Fill a clear jar with candy corn. Be sure to count the pieces as you place them in the jar.
2. As each guest arrives, have the guest write his or her name on a piece of paper along with an estimate of how many pieces of candy are in the jar.
3. During the party announce the name of the person who came closest to the actual number without going over. Award this person the jar of candy.

Witches, Ghosts, and Black Cats

1. Before the party guests arrive you will need to prepare for this game.
2. Cut from construction paper: five orange witches' hats, five white ghosts, and five black cats.
3. On each of the five hats write one letter to spell WITCH. On each of the white ghosts write one letter to spell GHOST. And on each of the black cats write one letter to spell BLACK.
4. Before the guests arrive, hide these shapes around the room.

HIDE THESE SHAPES:

NAME TAGS

5. You will also need to make additional shapes of each to be used as name tags.
6. As the guests arrive, give each person either a hat, a ghost, or a cat name tag to wear. Alternate the shapes that are given out.
7. Tell the guests that you will explain the purpose of the name tags later during the party.

8. When it is time to play the game, tell the players that all the witches' hats form one team, all the ghosts form a second team, and all the cats a third team.
9. Explain that each team will have to find five of their shapes hidden in the room in order to spell their words, WITCH, GHOST, and BLACK.
10. The first team to find all five shapes and arrange them in order wins.

Spin Your Fortune

1. Follow these directions to make a fortune wheel:
   a. Cut a circle at least 12'' in diameter from cardboard.
   b. Cut an arrow from cardboard and attach it to the center of the circle with a brad fastener. Turn the arrow several times so that it will easily spin when it is time to play.
   c. Divide the circle into twelve (or more) sections by drawing lines.
   d. In each section write the name of a profession. Use the suggestions listed below or use your own ideas.
2. Give each guest a chance to spin the arrow. The word the arrow points to tells the player's future profession.
3. The guest then receives a token gift that represents their fortune.
   Professions and tokens to use:
   doctor—bandage
   mechanic—screw
   hair stylist—comb
   carpenter—nail
   writer—pencil
   artist—paint brush
   farmer—potato
   locksmith—key
   chef—spoon
   florist—flower
   architect—ruler
   teacher—chalk

CHAPTER FOUR

THANKSGIVING

The year has turned its circle,
The seasons come and go.
The harvest is all gathered in
And chilly north winds blow.

Orchards have shared their treasures,
The fields, their yellow grain,
So open wide the doorway—
Thanksgiving comes again!

Each year toward the end of November when you are preparing for your Thanksgiving feast, do you realize that you are making ready for one of the oldest celebrations in the world?

Thanksgiving is annually celebrated by families in the United States and Canada. But people all over the world have always set aside their own special days for feasting and prayer to show gratitude for the many blessings they have received during the year.

For centuries people have held harvest festivals after all their crops are gathered in. The ancient Greeks celebrated festivals throughout the year to give thanks to their many gods and goddesses. For hundreds of years the people of England and Europe held harvest-home festivals. This time of feasting, singing, and dancing was an expression of the people's gratitude for the good harvest in anticipation of the long, cold winter months.

The first American Thanksgiving was celebrated in New England less than a year after the Pilgrims settled Plymouth colony in Massachusetts. The first winter brought many hardships, but there was new hope the following summer and autumn with the good harvest. Now there would be plenty of food. The date of the first Thanksgiving is not known exactly, but there was much feasting among the Pilgrims and their newly found friends, Chief Massasoit and the Wampanoag Indians, during the fall of 1621. Today Thanksgiving is observed as a legal federal holiday on the fourth Thursday of November.

THE SYMBOLS OF THANKSGIVING

Many of the symbols we use at Thanksgiving time reflect that first Thanksgiving.

Wild game was eaten at the first Thanksgiving feast. Since the woods were filled with game such as wild turkeys, the *turkey* has become a traditional food for Thanksgiving, even though deer and fish were probably prepared for the first Thanksgiving as well.

Squanto, an Indian friend to the Pilgrims, showed them how to plant *corn*, which became a very important food source. The Indians also introduced the Pilgrims to a real treat, popcorn. Other crops such as *pumpkins* and various *gourds* grew in plenty. The Pilgrims quickly learned to prepare and eat all these strange foods. Harvest tables are often decorated with the colorful gourds.

A *cornucopia* is a receptacle shaped like a horn or a cone. It is usually filled with many fruits and vegetables and signifies abundance. This symbol decorates dining tables at Thanksgiving feasts.

We often associate Pilgrim hats and Indian headdresses with the first Thanksgiving feast. We use these symbols to decorate cards, place mats, paper napkins and tablecloths, and napkin holders for modern-day Thanksgiving tables.

The *Mayflower*, the ship used by the first Pilgrims to travel across the Atlantic, is seen today in miniature on our Thanksgiving tables. Even though this rather small ship was the means for a new life of freedom for these people, it was by no means a luxury liner. The journey across the ocean was difficult in cramped quarters.

PARTY PLANS

INVITATIONS

Turkey Invitations

Materials

Brown, red, orange, and yellow construction paper
Scissors, Glue
Felt-tip pens

Directions

1. For each invitation, cut a turkey shape from a piece of construction paper, 6″ × 9″ (15 × 23 cm) in size.
2. Cut four large feathers and some smaller feathers from red, yellow, and orange construction paper.
3. Glue the feathers on the turkey as shown in the illustration.
4. On the turkey's body, write a verse.
5. On the colorful feathers write the time, place, and date of the party.
6. Make a turkey invitation for each guest.

Scroll Party Announcements

Materials

Brown paper bags
Black felt-tip pens
Scissors
Yarn or ribbon

Directions

1. For each scroll, cut the front or back from a brown paper bag. Cut jagged edges.
2. With a black felt-tip pen, write each party invitation on a sheet from the bag. Write in fancy calligraphy, if possible.
3. Write a message on the paper bag parchment.
4. Roll the invitation and tie it with yarn or ribbon.
5. Hand deliver each invitation to your friends.

TABLE DECORATIONS

Autumn Leaf Mats

Materials

    Red, orange, yellow, and brown construction paper, 12″ × 18″ (30 × 45 cm) in size
    Scissors
    Felt-tip pens

Directions

1. For each place mat, cut a large leaf from a 12″ × 18″ (30 × 45 cm) sheet of construction paper. Use fall colors.

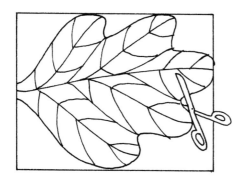

2. Draw details on the leaf with a felt-tip pen.
3. Make a place mat for each guest. You may want to write the guest's name on the mat. Alternate the different colored leaves as you set the table.

Gobbler Napkin Rings

Materials

    Brown, red, orange, yellow construction paper
    Scissors
    Glue
    Felt-tip pens

Directions

1. For each gobbler napkin ring, cut the following from construction paper:

body: a strip of brown, 8″ × 3″ (20 × 7½ cm); head: a strip of brown, 4″ × 1″ (10 × 3 cm); feet: 2 strips of orange, 2″ × 1″ (5 × 3 cm); beak: a strip of orange, ½″ × ¼″ (2 × 1 cm). Cut feathers from red, orange, and yellow paper. Cut a wattle from red paper.

2. Form rings with the strips for the body and head. Glue the ends. Then glue the head to the body.
3. Glue the beak and the wattle on the head. Color eyes on the face with a felt-tip pen.
4. Glue the feet on the bottom of the body.
5. Glue the feathers on the back.
6. Insert a napkin inside the largest ring.
7. Make one gobbler napkin ring for each guest.

Headdress Place Cards

Materials

   Construction paper (a variety of
      colors)
   Scissors
   Glue
   Felt-tip pen

Directions

1. For each headdress place card, cut a strip of construction paper 1″ × 6″ (3 × 15 cm).
2. Write the guest's name in the center of the strip and decorate around the name.
3. Then form a ring with the strip and glue the ends.

4. Cut three or more feathers, about 2″ (5 cm) long, from different colors of construction paper.

5. Glue the feathers to the front of the band.
6. Make a headdress place card for each guest.

Pine Cone Turkey Centerpiece

Materials

   Large pine cones
   Construction paper
   Scissors
   Glue
   Felt-tip pen

Directions

1. Cut a turkey head from red construction paper. Draw eyes, using a felt-tip pen. Cut a small beak from yellow construction paper and glue onto the head.
2. Cut a half-circle, about 7″ (18 cm) in diameter, from brightly colored paper (yellow, blue, orange). This half-circle will be the tail feathers. Cut points along the outer edge of the circle as shown in the illustration. Use a felt-tip pen to make markings resembling feathers.

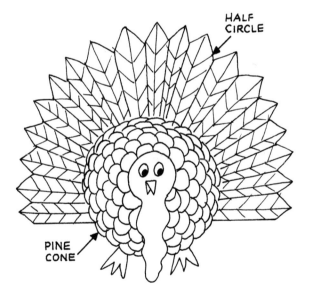

3. Cut two feet from orange construction paper.
4. Glue the head on the front of the pine cone. Glue the tail feathers on the back, and the feet on the bottom toward the front.

[33]

Miniature Mayflower Centerpiece

Materials

Brown construction paper, 12″ × 18″ (30 × 45 cm)

Cardboard tube from paper towels or wax paper

White paper, Drinking straws

Scissors, Glue

Directions

1. For each ship, take one sheet of brown construction paper and fold in half with the 12″ sides meeting.

2. With the fold at the top of the paper, draw the outline of the Mayflower.

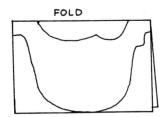

FOLD

3. While the paper is still folded, cut out the ship.

4. Take a piece of cardboard tubing, or make a tube by rolling a piece of construction paper, and place the tube between the sides of the ship at the bottom.

5. For the ship's masts, cut sails, 2″ to 3″ (5 to 8 cm) tall. Glue one or two sails to a drinking straw. Use three straws in all for the masts.

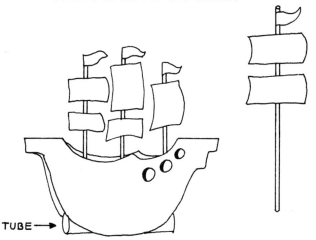

TUBE →

6. Glue small flags at the top of the masts if you wish.

7. Poke three small holes in the tube at the base of the ship.

8. Insert a mast in each hole.

PARTY FAVORS

Tubes of Goodies

Materials

Tubes from paper towels or wax paper

Construction paper (if no tubes are available)

Orange, yellow, or brown tissue paper

Candy and nuts

Yarn

Directions

1. Cut the tubes into lengths of 6″ (15 cm).

2. If no tubes are available, cut pieces of construction paper that are 6″ × 4″ (15 × 10 cm). Form a cylinder by rolling the paper from the 6″ (15 cm) side and taping or gluing the end.

3. Fill each tube with candy and nuts.

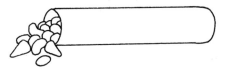

4. Cut a piece of orange, yellow, or brown tissue paper to wrap around each tube.

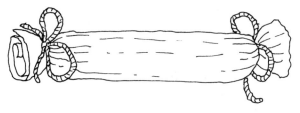

5. Tie the ends with yarn bows.

6. Make a party favor for each guest.

[34]

Pilgrim Hats

Materials
- Black, white, and yellow construction paper
- Paper bags (lunch bag size)
- Stapler
- Glue
- Felt-tip pens
- Candy, nuts, dried fruit

Directions
1. Cut two Pilgrim Hats from black construction paper for each party favor. Make the hats about 5″ (12 cm) wide and 8″ (20 cm) tall.

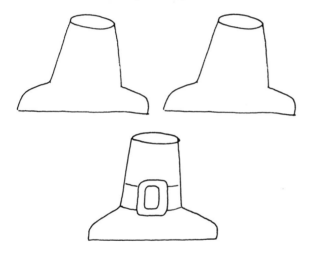

2. Add a white hat band and a yellow buckle on one hat. Write the guest's name on the hat.
3. Staple the bag between the two hats.

4. Fill the bag with candy, nuts, and fruit.
5. Make one party favor for each guest.

ROOM DECORATIONS

Balloon Turkeys

Materials
- Large, round balloons
- Yarn
- Construction paper
- Crayons or felt-tip pens
- Scissors
- Glue

Directions
1. Blow up each balloon and tie a piece of yarn to secure it.
2. Cut a double head, as shown in the illustration, two wings, tail feathers, and two feet from construction paper.
3. Color in any details with crayons or felt-tip pens.
4. Glue the turkey parts to the balloon body.
5. Suspend the turkeys from the ceiling.

Gourd Candle Holders

Materials
  Gourds of various colors, shapes,
    and sizes
  Candles
  Knife (table knife)

Directions
1. To make the gourd candle holders, cut a hole in each gourd. The holes must be wide and deep enough to fit the candles.
2. Set one candle in each gourd.
3. Place the gourd candle holders around the room.

Harvest Door Decoration

Materials
  Indian corn
  Ribbon
  Wire

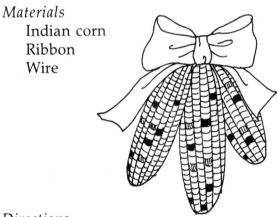

Directions
1. For each door decoration, take three cobs of Indian corn and tie them together with a thin wire.
2. Tie a pretty bow at the top.
3. Hang the harvest decoration on the door.

REFRESHMENTS

Cranberry Drinks

Serve any of the cranberry drinks that are available from the store. If you wish to serve a fancier drink, place a scoop of ice cream in the glass with the juice.

Iced Tea

Since people from England are so fond of tea, serve iced tea, which can easily be made by using a mix.

Turkey Sandwiches

  Sliced turkey
  White or rye bread
  Mayonnaise
  Mustard
  Lettuce, pickles, cheese

1. Place all the fixings for the sandwiches on plates.
2. Let the guests help themselves and make their own sandwiches.

Harvest Soup

  Cans of tomato soup (or beef or
    chicken broth)
  Fresh vegetables

To make the Harvest Soup a community effort do the following:
1. In the invitations that are sent, suggest that each guest bring one vegetable to the party.
2. At the time of the party, prepare the tomato soup as instructed on the cans. (You could also use beef or chicken stock.)
3. Have each guest wash and cut up the vegetable that was brought.
4. Have the cut vegetables put into the soup and simmer until tender. Noodles could also be added.

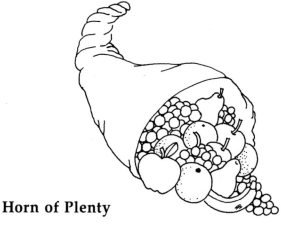

Horn of Plenty

Fresh fruits
Large brown paper bag

Make a horn of plenty for the table from which your guests can help themselves.
1. Take a large paper bag and twist the bottom of the bag to make a pointed end resembling the end of a cornucopia.
2. Set the bag (the horn of plenty) on its side and fill it with fresh fruits.

Harvest Apples

Apples
Caramel candies
Sticks
Cupcake papers
Construction paper
Tape or glue

1. Melt the caramels in a pan on low heat. (The package that the caramels come in will have the directions.) Stir often.
2. Place a stick in each apple.
3. Dip each apple into the caramel.
4. Allow the caramel apples to cool on buttered wax paper.
5. When cool and hardened, each apple should be put in a cupcake paper.
6. Cut a small Pilgrim hat or a feather from construction paper and glue or tape to the stick.

Pumpkin Harvest Squares

¾ cup (185 ml) all-purpose flour
¾ cup (185 ml) rolled oats
1 cup (250 ml) chopped nuts
½ cup (125 ml) margarine, softened
1 4-ounce (112-g) package of butterscotch pudding and pie-filling mix
1 teaspoon (5 ml) pumpkin pie spice
1 16-ounce (453.6 g) can of pumpkin
¾ cups or 1 14-ounce (435 ml) can of sweetened condensed milk
2 eggs

1. Preheat oven to 350°F (175°C).
2. Mix the first five ingredients in a large bowl.
3. Press into an ungreased 13″ × 9″ (32 × 23 cm) baking pan.
4. Combine the remaining ingredients, blending well.
5. Pour over the crust.
6. Bake 40 to 45 minutes, until a knife inserted in the center comes out clean.
7. Cool. Cut into bars.
8. You may wish to add whipped cream.
9. Makes about 15 squares.

Gobble-good Cookies

Large, round cookies (purchase from a store)
Vanilla wafers
Prepared chocolate icing in a can
Candy corn
Cinnamon candies
Raisins

1. Frost each large cookie with chocolate icing.
2. Place candy corn around the outer edge of one half of the cookie for tail feathers.
3. Frost the vanilla wafers, one per large cookie. Place one vanilla wafer on the large cookie for the head.
4. Attach a piece of candy corn for the beak.
5. Place some cinnamon candies under the beak for the wattle.

6. Place a raisin on the head for the eye.
7. Decorate one cookie for each guest.

Harvest Cream

Chocolate ice cream
Candy corn

1. Place a scoop of chocolate ice cream in each dish.
2. Sprinkle candy corn on top.

GAMES

Scavenger Hunt

1. Divide your party guests up into pairs or small teams.
2. Give each team a list of items they must find.
3. Include items that relate to the season, such as a red leaf, a nut, a corn kernel, a twig, and a picture of a ship.
4. The first team to bring all the items back within a given time period wins.

Cornucopia Memory Game

1. The starting player names something he or she will put in the cornucopia that begins with the letter *a*, such as *apples.*
2. The second player repeats what has been said and adds something that begins with the letter *b.*
3. The game continues, using the letters of the alphabet consecutively.
4. You may omit the more difficult letters of the alphabet.

Cranberry String Contest

1. You will need threaded needles and bowls of fresh cranberries for this game.
2. Give each player a threaded needle and set the players near a bowl of cranberries.
3. At the signal to begin, the players are to string as many cranberries as they can during the playing time. (Allow about 5 minutes.)
4. The player having the most cranberries on the string is the winner.

Menu Mix-up

1. Give each player a piece of paper, having a list of foods for a Thanksgiving feast. However, the letters in each word should be scrambled.
2. The letters must be unscrambled and the words rewritten within a certain amount of time. (Allow about 10 minutes.)
3. The first player to unscramble all the words wins the grand prize. All other players who have correct answers win prizes also.
   Use such words as:
   krutye (turkey)
   nrcbryrae (cranberry)
   fustgnif (stuffing)
   miuppnk ipe (pumpkin pie)
   uqashs (squash)
   vgrya (gravy)
   mays (yams)
   atpootes (potatoes)
   rcators (carrots)

Barter Game

The Indians and the Pilgrims had to barter with each other to obtain the different items they needed.

1. Purchase small party gifts and wrap them in paper.
2. At the time of the game, give each player a wrapped surprise.
3. Allow the player to feel and shake the package, but not to open it.
4. If the player does not wish to keep the gift, he or she must barter with another guest in order to exchange it.
5. Allow about 10 minutes for the bartering.
6. At the end of the time period, each player may keep the wrapped item he or she has. Then the gifts may be opened.

Turkey Hunt

1. For this game the players will work in pairs.
2. You will need one balloon turkey for each pair of players.

3. You can make the balloon turkeys as described on page 35 or use plain balloons.
4. Two sets of players will compete at one time.
5. One player from each pair will be blindfolded. This player will be given a safety pin.
6. The second player of each pair will place the balloon turkey somewhere in the room.
7. At the signal to start the competition, the two blindfolded players are turned around two or three times while their partners are placing the balloons in the room.
8. The unblindfolded players are to guide their blindfolded partners to the hidden turkeys by making gobble noises. The players cannot touch each other.
9. When a blindfolded player has found a balloon turkey, he or she is to pop it with the safety pin.
10. The first pair to catch and pop the turkey wins. Then continue the game with two new sets of partners.

CHAPTER FIVE

CHRISTMAS

Green and red trim everywhere,
Silver bells, shiny and bright,
People bustling throughout the town,
What a happy, wintry sight.

Merry singing fills the air,
Bringing thoughts of holiday cheer.
Christmas has come once again.
It's our favorite time of year.

Christmas means many things to many people. But the simple message that this feast brings to everyone is love. Christmas is a joyful time for family gatherings, cheerful songs, gift giving, and visiting friends. Countries all over the world have their own traditional Christmas festivities. The sights, sounds, and symbols of Christmas have evolved from centuries of celebrating the birth of Christ.

THE SYMBOLS OF CHRISTMAS

The *creche*, a representation of the Nativity scene, is a familiar one in homes and churches at Christmas. Even though artists have interpreted the scene differently over the years, and though there are different versions of the story, the creche usually includes Mary, Joseph, the Christ Child, angels, the Three Wise Men, shepherds, and sheep and donkeys.

According to the Bible, an angel appeared to the shepherds and announced the birth of Christ. *Angels* are frequently pictured guarding the manger.

The branches of the *evergreen tree* remain green throughout the year. People of long ago took this to be a spiritual sign and believed that this tree would protect them from harm and even death. So people began bringing the green trees into their homes. The Christmas tree decorated with colorful ornaments and bright lights is a common sight during the Christmas season.

The circle has always been a symbol of everlasting life, a symbol of God. The *Christmas wreath*, which is circular in shape, has this same religious symbolism but has also become a welcome sign for visitors on the doors of homes that they go to during this season of good will.

Depending on the custom of a particular country, small presents were often put in shoes, hung on trees, or wrapped and placed under a Christmas tree. The *Christmas stocking*, hung from the mantel, has become a popular tradition. Small wrapped packages as well as fruit and nuts are often found in these stockings on Christmas morning.

The *Christmas Star*, which is said to have been the guiding light for the Wise Men in their search for the newborn Christ child, is a popular holiday symbol. The place of honor for this star is often at the top of the Christmas tree.

Santa Claus is that jolly, white-bearded, plump man dressed in a red suit who travels through the air in his reindeer-drawn sleigh on Christmas Eve, delivering presents to people all over the world. This special man is also known as San Nicholaas, Nikolaus, Klaus, or Claus. Santa Claus can be traced to a real person, an early Christian, Nicholas, the bishop of Myra in Asia Minor. He was a kindly man who, according to legend, always helped people in need.

Christmas is a time for *gift giving*. Family and friends are remembered on this day with presents given with love.

PARTY PLANS

INVITATIONS

Snowflake Print Invitations

Materials
- Blue construction paper
- White tempera paint
- Paint brushes
- Green pepper
- Knife
- Felt-tip pens
- Scissors

Directions:
1. To make each card, cut a sheet of construction paper into a piece 9″ × 6″ (23 × 15 cm) in size.
2. Fold the piece of paper in half with the 6″ (15 cm) sides meeting.

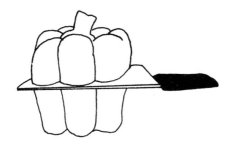

3. To decorate the card with a snowflake print, you will need to cut a green pepper in half. Cut crosswise, from side to side as shown in the illustration. The inside of each half can be used to make the snowflake prints.
4. With a brush, coat the inside of one pepper with white tempera paint.

5. Press the pepper firmly on the front side of the blue construction paper card. The print will resemble a snowflake.

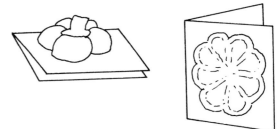

6. Inside the invitation write a verse.
7. Make one invitation for each guest.

Christmas has come again
A time of joy and cheer.
A party is planned to
celebrate.
We hope you'll join us here.

Time —
Place —
Date —

TABLE DECORATIONS

Season's Greetings Place Mats

Materials

White construction paper, 12″ × 18″
(30 × 45 cm) in size
Red and green crayons or felt-tip
pens, Scissors

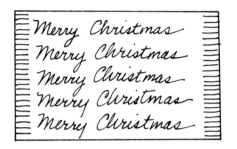

Directions

1. Use one piece of white construction paper for each place mat. With crayons or felt-tip pens, color a 1″ (3 cm) border of red along one 12″ (30 cm) side and a border of green along the other 12″ (30 cm) side.
2. Use scissors to fringe the borders.
3. With red and green crayons or felt-tip pens, write *Merry Christmas* on the mat, repeating the words several times, alternating red and green.
4. Make one place mat for each guest.

Snowflake Print Mats

Materials

Red, green, or blue construction paper, 12″ × 18″ (30 × 45 cm)
Green pepper, White tempera paint
Paint brushes, Scissors, Knife

Directions

1. For each place mat, use one sheet of construction paper.
2. Cover the paper with snowflake prints made with the green pepper. Directions for making these prints can be found on page 43.

Santa Napkin Rings

Materials

Red and white construction paper
Red napkins
Scissors
Glue
Crayons or felt-tip pens
Cotton (optional)

Directions

1. For each napkin ring, cut a strip of paper 6″ × 1½″ (15 × 4 cm) from red construction paper.
2. Form a ring with the strip, and glue the ends.

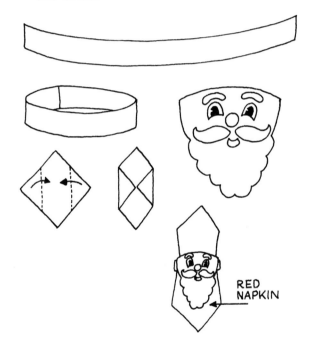

RED NAPKIN

3. Cut out a Santa face from white construction paper. Use a piece of paper, approximately 4″ × 3″ (10 × 7½ cm).
4. Color details on the face with crayons or felt-tip pens. Glue on cotton for the beard, if you wish.
5. Fold the two opposite points of a napkin to the back, forming a point at the top and bottom.
6. Slip the napkin inside the ring. The red napkin becomes Santa's hat.

Rudolph Place Cards

Materials

White construction paper or 3" X 5" (7½ X 13 cm) index cards
Brown and yellow construction paper
Felt-tip pens, Scissors, Glue

Directions

1. For each place card, use an index card or cut a piece of white paper to this size.
2. Fold the card in half lengthwise, having the 5" (13 cm) sides meet.
3. Write the name of the guest on one half.
4. For the other half, you will make Rudolph the Red-nosed Reindeer's head.
5. From brown construction paper, cut a triangle that is 1" (3 cm) on each side.
6. Glue the triangle onto the card as shown in the illustration. Color in eyes and a red nose.

7. Cut two antlers from yellow construction paper and glue onto the head.
8. Make one place card for each guest.

Evergreen Place Cards

Materials

Green construction paper
Scissors
Felt-tip pens

Directions

1. For each place card, cut two pieces of green construction paper, 5" X 4" (13 X 10 cm).
2. Fold one piece of construction paper in half lengthwise, with the 5" (13 cm) sides meeting.
3. Draw half of an evergreen tree as shown in the illustration. The points are drawn away from the fold.
4. Cut out the tree, being careful not to cut on the fold.

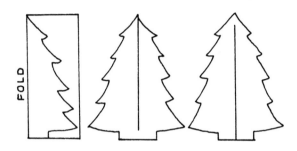

5. Then use the cut-out tree as a pattern to draw and cut out a second tree. You will have two trees of the same size.
6. To put the trees together, cut a slit down the center of one tree, cutting from the bottom up to within ½" (3 cm) of the top.
7. With the second tree, cut the slit from the top down to within ½" (3 cm) of the bottom.
8. Color dots on the trees with felt-tip pens, and write the guest's name on the tree.
9. Put the tree together by slipping one onto the other. The tree will stand by itself.

Cone Candle Centerpiece

Materials
Cardboard (corrugated cardboard is best)
Small pine cones
Glue
Scissors
Red or green ribbon
Red or green candles

Directions
1. For each candle holder, cut a circle from cardboard that is about 4″ (10 cm) in diameter.
2. In the center of the circle cut a hole just large enough for a candle to fit.
3. If your cardboard is too thin, you may need to stack and glue two or three circles so the candle will stand.

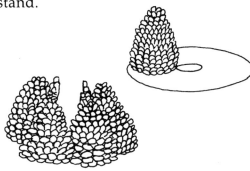

4. Glue several small pine cones on the cardboard around the hole.
5. Attach a small red or green ribbon.
6. Insert the candle. (In order for the candle to stand upright, you may need to put a little clay under it.)

PARTY FAVORS

Christmas Cups

Materials
Cupcake papers
Green construction paper
Scissors
Stapler
Felt-tip pens
Candies and nuts

Directions
1. For each party favor, cut a holly leaf from green construction paper. Make the leaf about 3″ (8 cm) long.
2. On each holly leaf write Merry Christmas, but write the words in a foreign language:
   French: *Joyeux Noel* (zhwah-YUH noh-EHL)
   German: *Frohliche Weihnachten* (FRUH-lee-kheh VIGH-nahkh-t 'n)
   Spanish: *Felices Navidades* (feh-LEE-thes NA-vee-DAH-des)
   Italian: *Buon Natale* (bwohn nah-TAH-leh)
   Norwegian: *God Jul* (god yool)
   Portuguese: *Felez Natal* (feh-LEES nah-TAHL)
   Hawaiian: *Mele Kalikimaka* (MEH-leh kah-lee-kee-MAH-kah)
   (It is not necessary to write the pronunciations too, but have them on hand so that the words can be correctly pronounced.)
3. Staple each holly leaf on a cupcake paper.
4. Fill the cups with candy and nuts.
5. Make one favor for each guest.

Santa Surprises

Materials
- Red and white construction paper
- Green posterboard
- Cotton, Yarn, Paper cups
- Small candy canes, Tape, Scissors
- Glue, Stapler, Hole puncher

Directions

1. Cut the bottom out of each paper cup.
2. Cover each cup with red construction paper. To do this, make a pattern to trace on the paper.
3. Use a cup for the pattern. Cut the bottom from the cup and cut up the side. Open and flatten out the cup.
4. Trace the cup pattern on red construction paper. You will need one pattern cut from red construction paper for every cup you wish to use.
5. Wrap a piece of red paper around a cup and staple or glue in place.
6. Next, from red construction paper cut circles about 6'' (15 cm) in diameter.
7. Cut each circle in half. You will need one half-circle for each Santa's hat.
8. Curve the half-circle around to form a cone shape and staple or glue together.
9. Glue cotton around the rim of the hat and a cotton ball on top.
10. Next, cut pieces of green posterboard that are 4'' × 6'' (10 × 15 cm) in size. These will be sleighs.
11. Punch two holes on one of the shorter sides and string a piece of yarn through them. These will be reins.
12. Tape a candy cane along each of the 6'' (15 cm) sides for runners on the sleigh.
13. Tape Santa's body (turn the covered paper cup rim-side down) onto the sleigh.
14. Glue a white mustache on the front of the cup.
15. Fill the cup with candies, nuts, and raisins.
16. Place the hat on Santa's head.
17. Put a Santa by each place setting.

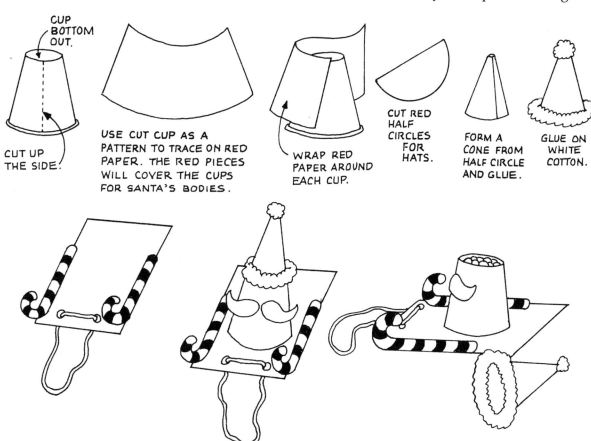

CUP BOTTOM OUT.

CUT UP THE SIDE.

USE CUT CUP AS A PATTERN TO TRACE ON RED PAPER. THE RED PIECES WILL COVER THE CUPS FOR SANTA'S BODIES.

WRAP RED PAPER AROUND EACH CUP.

CUT RED HALF CIRCLES FOR HATS.

FORM A CONE FROM HALF CIRCLE AND GLUE.

GLUE ON WHITE COTTON.

ROOM DECORATIONS

Personalized Stockings

Materials
- Construction paper, 12″ × 18″ (30 × 45 cm)
- Scissors
- Glue
- Crayons or felt-tip pens
- Small gifts or treats

Directions
1. For each Christmas stocking, fold a piece of construction paper in half, with the 18″ (45 cm) sides meeting.
2. Draw a stocking shape with the back of the stocking against the fold.
3. Cut the stocking out (on the dotted lines as shown in the illustration).
4. Glue the side and bottom of the stocking, leaving the top open.
5. Decorate each stocking, using crayons or felt-tip pens. You may want to add glitter, sequins, cotton, and other decorations. Write the party guest's name on the stocking.
6. Fill the stocking with surprise presents or tasty goodies.

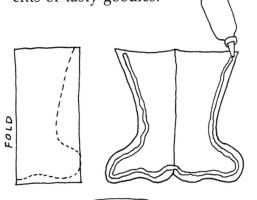

Snow People Mobiles

Materials
- Construction paper
- Yarn
- Tape
- Glue
- Felt-tip pens

Directions
1. For each mobile, cut three pairs of circles from white construction paper: the first pair of circles for the head, 2″ (5 cm) in diameter; the second pair of circles for the midsection, 3″ (8 cm) in diameter; the third pair of circles for the bottom, 4″ (10 cm).
2. On one of the smallest circles, color in eyes, nose, and mouth with crayons or felt-tip pens.
3. On one of the middle-size circles, color buttons.

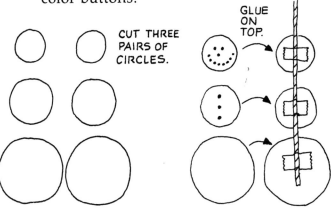

CUT THREE PAIRS OF CIRCLES.

GLUE ON TOP.

4. Tape or glue a long piece of yarn across three of the circles, leaving space in between. Glue the other three circles on top with the yarn in between.
5. Cut a hat from construction paper, and glue it to the head. Make different hats for each snow person (baseball caps, top hats, hats with flowers, hard hats, police officer hats, nurse's caps, etc.).
6. Suspend the mobile from the ceiling or hang in a window.

REFRESHMENTS

Holiday Soda

Ginger ale
Cherry and lime Kool Aid
Ice cube trays

1. Make the cherry and lime Kool Aid according to the directions on the package. Pour into ice cube trays.
2. Allow the Kool Aid to freeze.
3. When the cubes are frozen, put a few green and red cubes into a tall glass and fill the glass with ginger ale.

Holiday Egg Nog

2 cups (500 ml) cold milk
2 eggs
4 teaspoons (20 ml) sugar
1 teaspoon (5 ml) vanilla
Ground nutmeg

1. Put all the ingredients except the nutmeg into a blender.
2. Cover and blend at a slow speed until smooth.
3. Pour into serving glasses and top with nutmeg.
4. You may wish to add a dab of whipped cream or even a scoop of ice cream.

Cranberry Salad

1 16-ounce (473 ml) can of whole cranberries
1 apple, chopped
1 20-ounce (600 ml) can of crushed pineapple
½ cup (125 ml) chopped walnuts
1 cup (250 ml) sour cream
Lettuce leaves

1. Mix all the ingredients together.
2. Pour into a 9″ × 12″ (23 × 30 cm) pan.
3. Place the pan in the freezer for about three hours.
4. Remove the pan from the freezer. Cut the frozen salad into squares and serve on a lettuce leaf.
5. Makes about 12 servings.

Holiday Pizzas

English muffins, cut in half
Pizza sauce
Mozzarella cheese
Garnishes for the pizzas: pepperoni, olives, mushrooms, green pepper, onions, etc.

1. Coat several muffin halves with pizza sauce.
2. Invite all the party guests to put the garnishes of their choice on top, ending with the cheese.
3. Place the pizzas in an oven at 350° F (175° C) and bake for about 15 minutes or until the cheese is melted.

Christmas Cheese Ball

1 cup (250 ml) grated cheddar cheese
1 8-ounce (236 ml) package cream cheese
½ teaspoon (2.5 ml) Worcestershire sauce
chopped olives with pimientos
½ cup (125 ml) chopped nuts

1. Allow the cream cheese to soften at room temperature.
2. Mix with the cheddar cheese, Worcestershire sauce, and olives.
3. Form the cheese mixture into a ball and roll it in the chopped nuts.
4. Top the cheese ball with a red or green cherry.
5. Refrigerate until ready to use.
6. Serve with crackers.

Christmas Cherry Bars

½ cup (62 ml) butter or margarine, softened
1 cup (250 ml) sugar
2 eggs
1¼ cups of biscuit mix (310 ml)
1 cup (250 ml) chopped walnuts or pecans
1 cup (250 ml) dates, chopped
½ cup (125 ml) maraschino cherries, drained and chopped

1. Mix butter, sugar, and eggs.
2. Stir in the biscuit mix.
3. Fold in the nuts, dates, and cherries.
4. Spread the mixture into a greased 13″ × 9″ × 2″ (33 × 23 × 5 cm) baking pan.
5. Bake at 350° F (175° C) for 30 minutes.
6. Cool. Cut into squares.
7. Makes about 3 dozen.

GAMES

Trim the Tree

1. Trimming a Christmas tree can be an activity that you may wish to do during the party.
2. To trim the tree the old-fashioned way, have the party guests string popped corn and cranberries. Pop the corn beforehand and have plenty of needles and thread handy.
3. You could also attach ribbons to pine cones and hang those on the tree.
4. To complete the trimming of the tree, play the game Hidden Candy Canes.

Hidden Candy Canes

1. Before the party guests arrive, hide several candy canes around the room.
2. After the Christmas tree has been decorated with strings of popcorn and cranberries and pine cones, tell the guests that there are candy canes hidden all around the room.
3. At the signal to begin, have everyone search for the candy canes.
4. You may want to award a prize to the person who hangs the most candy canes on the tree.

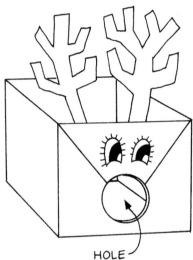

HOLE

Rudolph's Nose

1. Cover a box with brown paper, or use a box that is already brown.
2. Add eyes and some cardboard antlers as shown in the illustration.
3. Cut a large hole where the nose would be positioned.
4. Take four small paper bags, stuff them with newspaper, and tie the bags closed.
5. Give each player a turn at trying to toss the four bags into the reindeer's nose.
6. Keep score to see who tosses the most bags into Rudolph's nose.

Christmas Piñata

A popular part of the Mexican Christmas tradition is the piñata, a large decorated earthenware jar which is filled with candy, nuts, fruit, and small gifts, and hung from the ceiling. One child is blindfolded and given a stick with which to break the piñata. When the piñata bursts, all the children scramble to get a share of the goodies.

1. To make a simplified version of the piñata, fill a brown paper bag with treats and small gifts. Tie the bag with a string.
2. To decorate, glue strips of red and green crepe paper on the bag.
3. Suspend the bag from the ceiling.
4. Put all the guests' names in a box and draw a name out. This guest will be blindfolded and will try to break the piñata. When it bursts all the guests can pick up goodies.

Guessing Game

1. Write Christmas words on large pieces of paper, such as *Christmas tree, Santa Claus, reindeer, December 25, snow, winter, presents, North Pole, Rudolph,* and *sleigh ride.*
2. Pin one word on the back of one of the players.
3. Allow the other players to see the word.
4. The player who is "it" must ask the others questions that require yes or no answers in order to guess the word on the paper.
5. A maximum of eight questions can be asked.
6. Then a new player becomes "it" and a new word is used.
7. Each player who guesses the word correctly wins a prize.

Filling the Christmas Stocking

1. For this game you will need a die, sheets of paper, and crayons or felt-tip pens.
2. The object of the game is to see who can draw the stocking first.
3. Each player will take turns rolling the die once. A player must roll a 1 to begin the drawing. When a 1 is rolled, a player draws a stocking.
4. The illustrations show what detail is added with each roll.

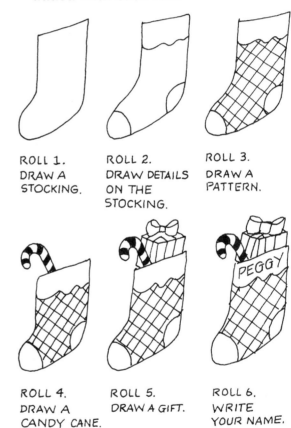

ROLL 1.
DRAW A
STOCKING.

ROLL 2.
DRAW DETAILS
ON THE
STOCKING.

ROLL 3.
DRAW A
PATTERN.

ROLL 4.
DRAW A
CANDY CANE.

ROLL 5.
DRAW A GIFT.

ROLL 6.
WRITE
YOUR NAME.

5. The details of the stocking must be drawn in numerical order. If a player rolls a number he or she cannot use, the player must wait until the next turn to roll again.
6. The first player to complete the drawing wins. The prize could be a real stocking filled with surprises.

CHAPTER SIX

HANUKKAH

Lighted Hanukkah candles
That give a warming glow
Remind us of a story
That happened long ago.

Singing and present giving
During days of eight
Make Hanukkah a joyous time
For us to celebrate.

Hanukkah is a Jewish holiday that is observed about the same time as Christmas, during the midwinter. It is an eight-day celebration that is a time for gift giving and parties. The feast is observed in memory of Judas Maccabaeus who over 2,000 years ago recaptured the temple at Jerusalem which had been taken by the Syrians.

Hanukkah is known as the "Festival of Lights" because candles are lighted in Jewish homes and in synagogues in observance of the feast.

THE SYMBOLS OF HANUKKAH

A special candle holder called a *menorah* holds one candle for each of the eight days plus one center candle called the Shamash (servant candle) from which all the others are lit.

The *dreidel* is a four-sided top that has a different Hebrew letter on each side. The letters are *N, G, H,* and *S,* but are written in Hebrew. Their symbolism means "a great miracle happened there." The children take turns spinning the dreidel. Depending on which letter comes up when the top stops spinning, the player either is rewarded with nuts and raisins or pays a forfeit.

The *Star of David,* a special six-sided star, is a symbol of the Jewish nation.

PARTY PLANS

INVITATIONS

Star of David Invitations

Materials

    Construction paper or sheets of stationery
    Felt-tip pens

Directions

1. For each invitation, cut a sheet of construction paper 9" × 6" (23 × 15 cm), or use a sheet of stationery that is any size.
2. Fold the piece of paper in half to use as the card.

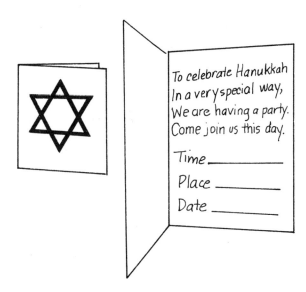

3. Draw a Star of David on the front of the card, using a felt-tip pen. Use a different color pen for each invitation.
4. Inside the card, write a verse.

Menorah Invitations

Materials

    Construction paper
    Scissors, Glue
    Felt-tip pens

Directions

1. For each invitation, cut a piece of construction paper 6" × 9" (15 × 23 cm).
2. Fold the paper in half for the card.
3. On the front, illustrate a menorah.
4. To make the candles for the menorah, use cut pieces of construction paper to glue on the card. Or simply draw them, using felt-tip pens.
5. If you choose to cut strips from construction paper, follow one of the designs shown in the illustrations or make up a design of your own.
6. Inside the invitation write a verse.

TABLE DECORATIONS

Hanukkah Place Mats

Materials

White construction paper, 12″ × 18″
(30 × 45 cm)
Crayons or felt-tip pens, Scissors

Directions

1. For each place mat, color a 1″ (3 cm) border along both of the 12″ sides of white construction paper. Use a different color for each side.
2. Use scissors to cut and fringe each colored side.
3. Use the same two colors to write *Happy Hanukkah* or *Shalom* across the mat, repeating the words several times and alternating the colors.
4. Make one place mat for each guest.

Star Napkin Rings

Materials

Yellow construction paper
Scissors, Glue, Glitter, Napkins

Directions

1. For each napkin ring, cut a strip from yellow construction paper 5″ × 1″ (13 × 3 cm).
2. Form a ring with the strip and glue.
3. Cut a Star of David from construction paper, about 2″ (5 cm) across.

4. Decorate the edges with glitter.
5. Glue the star on the ring.

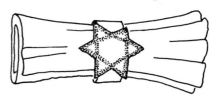

6. Insert a napkin.
7. Make one napkin ring for each guest.

Dreidel Napkin Ring

Materials

Construction paper
Felt-tip pens, Glue
Scissors, Napkins

Directions

1. Cut a strip of construction paper 5″ × 1″ (15 × 3 cm).
2. Fold the strip to make five 1″ (3 cm) square sections.

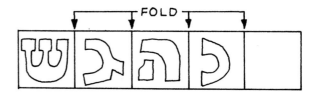

3. In each of the first four sections, draw one symbol found on the dreidel. (See the illustration.) Color the Hebrew letters with felt-tip pens.
4. To finish the square-shaped napkin ring, form a box by creasing each side, tucking the fifth square under the first, and gluing.
5. Insert a napkin in the napkin ring.
6. Make one napkin ring for each guest.

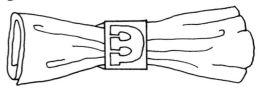

Hanukkah Place Cards

Materials

White construction paper or 3″ × 5″ (7½ × 13 cm) index cards
Yellow construction paper
Felt-tip pens or yarn, Scissors, Glue

Directions

1. Use an index card or cut a piece of white construction paper this size.
2. Fold the card in half lengthwise, having the 5″ (13 cm) sides meet.
3. Write the name of the guest on one half.
4. For the other half, cut a small Star of David from yellow construction paper and glue it onto the place card.

5. Trace around the edges of the star with felt-tip pens or put a thin line of glue along the outline and place yarn on the glue to outline the star.
6. Make one place card for each guest.

Menorah Centerpiece

Materials

Nine candles
Block of Styrofoam, 12″ × 2″ × 2″ (30 × 5 × 5 cm)
Knife, Ribbon, Glue, Holly greens

Directions

1. Use a dull table knife to cut a hole in the Styrofoam for each candle. To measure for the size of the hole, lightly press one of the candles into the Styrofoam at each place where a candle will be positioned. The candle will make an impression. Cut into the Styrofoam and hollow it out so the candle will fit inside.

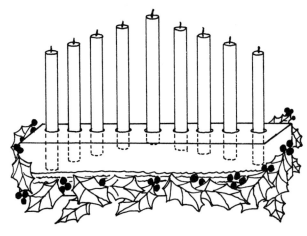

2. Make the four candles on either side of the center "servant" candle at different heights. To do this, cut deeper holes for the candles at each end. As you come closer to the center candle, make each hole less deep.
3. Put finishing touches on the candle holder by wrapping a ribbon around the block and gluing it in place. Place holly or other greens around the base.

PARTY FAVORS

Cups of Goodies

Materials

Cupcake papers
Construction paper
Stapler
Scissors
Felt-tip pens
  or crayons
Treats

Directions

1. Cut a small Star of David, about 2″ (5 cm) square, from yellow construction paper, and outline with a felt-tip pen or crayon.
2. Or cut a holly leaf from green construction paper and write the words *Happy Hanukkah* or *Shalom* on it.
3. Staple the star or the holly leaf onto the cupcake paper.
4. Fill the cup with treats.
5. Make one favor for each guest.

Miniature Dreidels

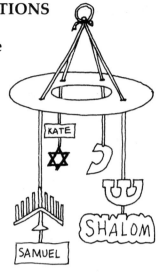

Materials

    Tagboard
    Scissors
    Tape
    Hole punch
    Carbon paper
    Felt-tip pens and pencils

Directions

1. For each miniature dreidel, you will need to make a box from tagboard.
2. Enlarge the pattern that is given so that each box is a 2″ (5 cm) square.
3. Trace the pattern on tagboard. Use a piece of carbon paper to mark the dotted lines.
4. Cut out the box.
5. Draw the symbols on the box.
6. Punch a hole in the center of the two designated squares.

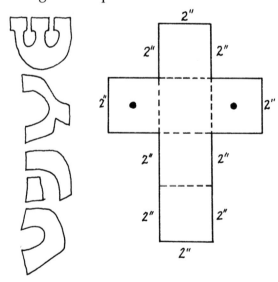

7. Fold the tagboard on the dotted lines to form the box. Tape the box together.
8. The sides with the holes are the top and bottom of the dreidel. Push a slightly sharpened pencil through the holes. This is the spinner.
9. Make a dreidel for each guest.
10. The directions for playing the game are given on page 60.

ROOM DECORATIONS

Hanukkah Mobile

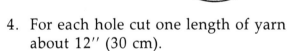

Materials

    Cardboard
    Yarn
    Construction
        paper or
        tagboard
    Felt-tip pens
        or crayons
    Scissors
    Pipe cleaner
    Tape

Directions

1. For each mobile, cut a ring from cardboard that is about 8″ (20 cm) in diameter and about 2″ (5 cm) wide.
2. Poke four or more holes in the ring.
3. Make a small ring from a pipe cleaner by twisting the ends together and forming a circle.

4. For each hole cut one length of yarn about 12″ (30 cm).
5. Pull one piece of yarn through each hole in the cardboard ring.
6. Gather the yarn pieces at the top and attach them to the ring.
7. You will have about 4″ (10 cm) of yarn from the pipe cleaner ring to the cardboard. The rest of each piece of yarn will hang below the ring.
8. From construction paper or tagboard, cut different Hanukkah symbols, such as Hebrew letters, the menorah, the Star of David, the word *Shalom*.
9. Color the symbols with felt-tip pens or crayons.
10. Tape the symbols to the yarn.

REFRESHMENTS

Green Float

Lime sherbet, Ginger ale

1. Put a large scoop of lime sherbet into each glass.
2. Fill the glass with ginger ale.

Latkes

2 pounds (.90 kg) potatoes, peeled
1 medium onion
½ cup (125 ml) boiling water
3 eggs
⅓ cup (80 ml) all-purpose flour
1 teaspoon (5 ml) salt
½ teaspoon (2.5 ml) baking powder
¼ teaspoon (1.2 ml) pepper
Salad oil for frying
Applesauce or sour cream

1. Grate the potatoes.
2. Remove 2 cups (500 ml) of potatoes and set aside.
3. Shred the onion.
4. Blend the potatoes and the onions in a large bowl.
5. Pour water over mixture and stir.
6. Beat in eggs, flour, salt, baking powder, pepper, and those potatoes that were set aside.
7. In a large skillet, heat ½" (2 cm) of oil. (An adult should supervise the frying.)
8. Drop potato batter by tablespoonsful into hot oil.
9. Fry until golden brown, turn and brown on other side.
10. Remove with a spatula and drain on paper towels.
11. Keep warm in a 200°F (93°C) oven while the others are frying.
12. Serve with applesauce or sour cream.
13. Makes about 20 pancakes.

Star of David Cake

Cake ingredients
1 cup (250 ml) all-purpose flour
½ teaspoon (2.5 ml) baking soda
½ teaspoon (2.5 ml) salt
¼ teaspoon (1.2 ml) baking powder
¼ cup plus two tablespoons (90 ml) water
¼ cup plus two tablespoons (90 ml) milk
¼ cup (60 ml) shortening
1 egg
½ teaspoon (2.5 ml) vanilla
2 unsweetened chocolate squares, melted and cooled

Icing
1 can of prepared icing
Cake decorations and candles

1. Heat the oven to 350°F (175°C).
2. Grease and flour a 9" (27 cm) square pan.
3. Beat all the cake ingredients in a large bowl for about three minutes.
4. Pour the batter into the pan.
5. Bake 30 to 35 minutes.
6. When the cake has cooled, cut it according to the directions to form the Star of David. Pieces 1 and 2 are put together to form the large center triangle. Pieces 3, 4, and 5 are smaller triangles that will form the three additional points. Place these against the three sides of the larger triangle.
7. Ice the entire cake.
8. Decorate with nuts, cherries, chocolate sprinkles, etc.

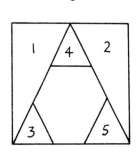 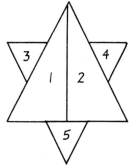

GAMES

Spin the Dreidel

1. The dreidel is a four-sided spinning top. Directions for making the dreidel are found on page 58.
2. The game can be played for any prize you wish, such as nuts, raisins, pennies, or candies. Every player begins the game with ten treats or pennies. Everyone puts one in the "kitty" to begin the game.
3. Everyone takes a turn spinning the dreidel. The Hebrew letter shown on the dreidel when it stops tells the player what to do.

 Nun
means you do nothing.

 Gimmel
means take all in the kitty.

 Hay
means take half.

 Sheen
means put a treat or a penny in the kitty.

4. Continue to play until one player has all the treats or pennies.

Dreidel Box

1. Cover a large cardboard box with paper. Remove the top.
2. Paint one dreidel symbol on each of the four sides.
3. Wrap several small gifts and tie a long piece of yarn to each.
4. Place the gifts inside the box and pull the pieces of yarn to the outside.

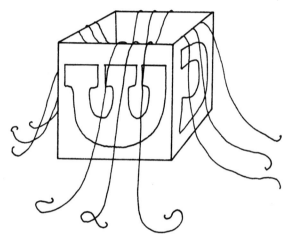

5. Put an equal number of strings coming out in front of each of the four Hebrew letters.
6. Using a dreidel, allow each guest to spin the top. The Hebrew letter shown on the dreidel will be the side of the surprise box from which the player will pull one piece of yarn.
7. Whatever present is at the end of that piece of yarn goes to the player.
8. If all the pieces of yarn happen to be gone from one particular side of the box, simply have the player spin again for another symbol.

OTHER BOOKS
TO READ

The following books are good references that you may find helpful in planning a holiday celebration. Some of the books will give interesting background information on the holidays we have been celebrating for years. The others give suggestions for party games, costumes, refreshments, and decorations. You will even find ideas for plays and costumes in a few.

Bradley, Virginia. *Holidays on Stage.* New York: Franklin Watts, 1983. Ideas for ten original short plays.

Chambers, Wicke, and Asher, Spring. *The Celebration Book of Great American Traditions.* New York: Harper & Row, 1983. Takes a look back into history and explains how many celebrations originated and how people continue to celebrate them today.

Christensen, Hedevig. *Stories About Our Holidays Told by Grandpas.* Ardmore, PA: Dorrance, 1973. Holiday traditions told in a folksy manner.

Corwin, Judith Hoffman. *Christmas Fun.* New York: Messner, 1982. A book of ideas for Christmas treats, gifts, cards, ornaments, and a bit about Christmas around the world.

_____. *Halloween Fun.* New York: Messner, 1983. A collection of Halloween tricks and treats including ideas for costumes, cookies, cards, cakes, and activities.

Drucker, Malka. *Hanukkah: Eight Nights, Eight Lights.* New York: Holiday House, 1980. An explanation of the popular Jewish celebration, Hanukkah.

Greene, Carol. *Holidays Around the World.* Chicago: Childrens Press, 1982. A look at holiday celebrations from countries all over the world.

Hopkins, Lee Bennett, ed. *Good Morning to You, Valentine.* New York: Harcourt Brace Jovanovich, 1976. A whimsical tribute to that special day in February through poetry.

_____. *Merrily Comes Our Harvest In.* New York: Harcourt Brace Jovanovich, 1978. A collection of poetry that celebrates the harvest feast of Thanksgiving.

McGovern, Ann. *Why It's a Holiday.* New York: Random House, 1960. Stories and explanations of several different holidays.

Myers, Robert J. *Celebrations.* New York: Doubleday, 1972. A book of celebrations of every kind.

Newman, Deborah. *Holiday Plays for Little Players.* Boston: Plays, 1957. A book of plays for children with holiday themes.

Parlin, John. *Patriot's Days.* Champaign, IL: Garrard, 1964. Stories of American patriots, customary holiday decorations, and interesting celebrations that have been observed through the years.

Perry, Margaret. *Holiday Magic.* New York: Doubleday, 1978. Many ideas along with step-by-step instructions for party ideas for every important holiday and a few in between.

Rockland, Mae Shafter. *The Hanukkah Book.* New York: Schocken Books, 1975. The history and celebration of the Jewish feast of Hanukkah.

Rockwell, Molly, ed. *Norman Rockwell's Christmas Book.* New York: Harry N. Abrams, 1977. A delightful collection of the artist's wonderful works along with interesting information explaining the celebration of Christmas in America.

INDEX